D0710139

COURAGEOUS
LIVING
BIBLE STUDY

Michael Catt Stephen Kendrick Alex Kendrick

as developed with

Nic Allen

B&H Publishing Group
Nashville, TN

Published by LifeWay Press® © Copyright 2011 Sherwood Baptist Church
© Copyright 2011 Sherwood Pictures, A Ministry of Sherwood Baptist Church, Albany, GA.
All rights reserved.

ISBN: 9781415872475 • Item: 005476022

Dewey Decimal Classification: 248.642
Subject Heading: Courage\Men\Leadership\Family Life

Courageous Living Bible Study is a resource for credit in the Christian Growth Study Plan.
Visit *www.lifeway.com/CGSP* for more information.

Photo credits: page 13, United States Marine Corps; pages 20 and 30, Todd Stone; page 23,
Truro Daily News; page 33, Billy Graham Evangelistic Association; page 43, EthnoGraphic Media

Unless otherwise noted, Scripture quotations are taken from the Holman Christian Standard
Bible®, copyright © 1999, 2000, 2002, 2003 by Holman Bible Publishers. Used by permission.
Scripture quotations marked NIV are taken from the Holy Bible, New International Version, copy-
right © 1973, 1978, 1984 by International Bible Society.

To order additional copies of this resource: Write LifeWay Church Resources Customer Service,
One LifeWay Plaza; Nashville, TN 37234-0113; Fax order to 615.251-5933; Phone
1.800.458.2772; E-mail to *orderentry@lifeway.com;* Order online at *www.lifeway.com*

Printed in the United States of America

Leadership and Adult Publishing, LifeWay Christian Resources,
One LifeWay Plaza, Nashville, TN 37234-0175

Contents

It takes courage to fight for my family.

It takes courage to value what matters most.

It takes courage to impact future generations.

It takes courage to stand with Christ.

About the Authors

Alex, Stephen, and Michael with Jim McBride (center back), the fourth member of Sherwood Pictures' leadership team.

Michael Catt is a husband, father of two grown daughters, and, since 1989, he has served as senior pastor of Sherwood Baptist Church, Albany, Georgia (*www.MichaelCatt.com*). With Jim McBride, Michael is also executive producer of Sherwood Pictures. The church's mission is "to touch the whole world with the whole Word, motivated by a passion for Christ and compassion for all people."

Stephen Kendrick is a husband, father of four, and associate pastor for Sherwood Baptist Church. Stephen oversees the church's prayer ministry and produces all Sherwood movies. In addition to this study, Stephen and Alex co-wrote the *The Love Dare* best seller, *The Love Dare Bible Study*, and the movie-release curriculum *Honor Begins at Home: The COURAGEOUS Bible Study* (fall 2011).

Alex Kendrick is a husband, father of six, and associate pastor for Sherwood Baptist Church. He is a speaker, actor, writer, and the director of all Sherwood movies. Alex acted as Grant Taylor in *FACING THE GIANTS* and as Adam Mitchell in *COURAGEOUS*.

Nic Allen is a husband, father of two girls, and pastor. After 10 years in student ministry at Rolling Hills Community Church in Franklin, Tennessee, he transitioned to family and children's ministry to focus on parents, specifically fathers.

Honor Begins at Home
About the Movie

Four men, one calling: to serve and protect. As law enforcement officers, Adam Mitchell, Nathan Hayes, and their partners in the sheriff's department, David Thomson and Shane Fuller, are confident and focused. They willingly stand up to the worst the streets have to offer.

While Adam is winning at work, he struggles to connect at home. He and his teenage son are running in different directions. Between Dylan's video games and late-night training runs, there seems to be little common ground between father and son. And while his young daughter is his pride and joy, Adam definitely doesn't share Emily's zest for life.

Nathan, who grew up not knowing his dad, has done all he can to break the cycle of fatherlessness in his family. Nathan's young sons look up to him, but his teenage daughter is turning away as she begins to attract the attentions of young men.

Shane struggles as a divorced father attempting to stay involved in his son's life and to get ahead financially. Young officer David is single, with a well-hidden past.

Spending time together is a value of these men who eagerly welcome a new friend, Javier, into their circle. Javier finds humor in life as he works diligently to make ends meet. Focused on God, Javier lovingly strives to provide for his wife and two young children.

When tragedy strikes, these men are left actively wrestling with their hopes, fears, faith, and fathering. Can a newfound urgency help these dads draw closer to God and to their children? How will their stories impact your family?

"But as for me and my household, we will serve the Lord" (Josh. 24:15, NIV).

IN THEATERS SEPTEMBER 30, 2011

www.courageousthemovie.com • *www.iamcourageous.com*

Introduction
Live a Courageous Life

The word *pandemic* describes a disease outbreak that is larger in scale than expected and covers a large geographical area, often crossing international borders. It is broader in scope than an epidemic and often more threatening. The influenza outbreak of 1918 claimed in excess of 20 million lives world-wide and could easily be described as pandemic.[1]

Studies today prove that children living without fathers are more likely to be poor and to endure significant emotional, educational, medical, and psycho-logical problems. Similar studies reveal that more than 24 million American children currently live without their biological fathers. That statistic is in excess of 36 percent of American children, making fatherlessness a problem of pandemic proportions.[2]

The only solution to this widespread problem is a return to biblical fatherhood: men of courage taking a powerful stand in their homes and communities to love, lead, and protect their children and thereby eliminating the problems associated with fatherlessness. In the *COURAGEOUS* movie, four men recognize this need and boldly answer the call to be better fathers.

While Adam Mitchell and fellow law-enforcement officers Nathan Hayes, David Thomson, and Shane Fuller consistently give their best on their job, "good enough" seems to be all they can muster as dads. But they're quickly discovering that their standard is missing the mark. They know that God desires to turn the hearts of fathers to their children, but their children are beginning to drift further and further away from them.

Will they be able to find a way to serve and protect those who are most dear to them?

As is the case with these four dads, taking the principles outlined in this Bible study and applying them to your life as a believer will take courage.

The *COURAGEOUS* movie and this Bible study sound the call for the:

- father who is always working and feels somewhat disconnected at home
- soldier who has been deployed for months and can't wait to engage with his wife and kids
- dad who is home on weekends but flies out every Monday morning to work out of town
- young guy whose relationship went too far too quickly and who became a dad too young
- divorced dad who becomes a full-time dad every other weekend and one month during the summer
- stepdad who lives full time with stepkids
- single mom raising three children while wearing both parent hats every day
- young man with a new wife waiting for the arrival of their first child
- mature father who looks back on his life with regrets and wants to now impact his grandkids
- dad who never knew his father and longs to discover how to lead his family well

This is a call for believers to take a courageous stand for the sake of their children and their future. This study is for you!

1. Martin I. Meltzer, Nancy J. Cox, and Keiji Fukuda, "The Economic Impact of Pandemic Influenza in the United States: Priorities for Intervention" [online] 2005 [cited 5 January 2011]. Available from the Internet: *http://www.cdc.gov/ncidod/eid/vol5no5/meltzer.htm*
2. "The Extent of Fatherlessness" [online] 2007 [cited 5 January 2011]. Available from the Internet: *http://www.fathers.com/content/index.php?option=com_content&task=view&id=336*

How to Use This Study

Courageous Living Bible Study is organized into sections and can be used for small-group or personal study. Allow 45 to 60 minutes for group sessions.

The introductory section of each study contains the story of a modern-day hero whose life exemplifies or grapples with the day's topic. Learners should read the excerpt and be prepared to note and apply transferable principles when prompted by questions during group discussion.

The Bible study DVD contains clips from the film *COURAGEOUS* to accompany each of the four sessions. Each clip is 1:30–4:00 minutes in length and is supported by discussion questions based on the principle illustrated.

This section is the primary focus of each session. Learners will read a portion of Scripture and be prompted by a summary section to discuss questions related to the Bible passage.

Finally, a lesson summary and a challenge to live courageously complete the session. A personal application point for all believers (Everyone) as well as one for parents (Dads and Moms), is followed by a closing prayer experience. The group facilitator should be sensitive to any nonbelievers in the group.

Ideally, LIVE is processed as a small group that has experienced all other parts of the session together. Yet, if your group prefers, some application can be done during the week (there is no designated homework). Some activities, such as the courage commitment scale in session 1, may be better done privately at home. However you do it, commit to make meaningful application within your context to courageous living and to building courageous families.

A Letter to Leaders

Thank you for answering the call to lead this small-group Bible study. Know that as we prepared this study, we were lifting you up and considering the incredible role you will play.

While this Bible study targets dads and a return to biblical fatherhood, the material is for all learners in your church whether or not they have children. Even without kids of their own, everyone has a physical father, and the relationship we have with our dads has powerful implications on how we operate as believers in Christ. This study is also important for the women in your group.

Perhaps you are doing this study as part of a larger churchwide campaign anticipating the release of *COURAGEOUS*. Perhaps your group has already seen the movie and is engaging this four-week study as a follow-up. Regardless of the timing of your study or the format of your class, this study has enormous potential to help reshape families in your church and community.

The words on these pages are not powerful nor are they part of a secret formula guaranteed to improve family relationships and to grow your church. But combined with the life-changing, living Word of God, this message can be an incredible tool that inspires dramatic revival in the hearts of believers and offers a solid gospel tool for nonbelievers.

You may be experiencing some fear about leading this study. Be courageous! You have not been called by God to facilitate this study because you are the perfect parent or have raised perfect children. You may not even be a parent. You are leading this study because God equips His people to do His work. Our prayer for you is that as you guide this study you'll see God working in your life in mighty ways and sense real Holy-Spirit power sustaining you.

The best way for you to prepare each week is to complete the study yourself. Be open and transparent with your group, honestly revealing areas in which you also struggle. Pray that God will direct your conversation and empower you to lead well, and He will! Thank you for answering this courageous call.

A Special Note to Women

Undoubtedly you entertained the question, "What's in this for me?" as a wife, mother, or woman of faith engaged in this study. You are not alone. The movie COURAGEOUS is first targeted at men. There is an unmistakable void of biblical fatherhood in this country and its effects are far-reaching. As a mom, you have a direct hand in raising sons who will one day be fathers as well as in raising daughters who will one day choose a man to marry who will serve as father to her children.

You have an incredible responsibility before you. Even if you don't have children, you have a father, and you know the effect that either his presence or his absence has had in your life. This study is not only an opportunity for you to unpack the relationship you have with your own dad but also an opportunity for you to draw closer to your Heavenly Father.

While we desperately need men to step up and be the fathers that God has called and equipped them to be, we also need women to understand that call and to provide the necessary support and daily encouragement to make it a reality for our families. Thank you for recognizing the value of this study and for engaging it with an open heart and open mind. There is a specific application portion in each session just for you.

Our prayer for you as you engage in this study is that you will be drawn closer to the heart of God and His call on your life to be a courageous believer!

Guidelines for Small Groups

The following keys will help ensure that your group Bible study experience is as meaningful and impactful as possible. *Leader:* During the first meeting go over all four and ask each participant to commit to the guidelines.

Confidentiality

As you dive into small-group Bible study, members will be prompted to share thoughts and feelings related to the family they were raised in as well as the family they are forging now. All of these expressions are made out of trust and should be kept with the strictest confidence by the group.

Respect

As trust forms and participants begin to open up about their personal and family struggles, it often becomes easy to offer advice. Scripture teaches us to be quick to listen and slow to speak (Jas. 1:19). Listening is a key to respect. Even well-meaning advice can be ill-received if it is shared too quickly or before someone has full understanding.

It is important that participants commit to respecting one another's thoughts and opinions and to providing a safe place for those thoughts and opinions to be shared without fear of judgment.

Preparation

To get the most out of this Bible study, each group member should attend group meetings having read through the study and answered questions, ready to discuss the material. Each participant can respect the contribution of other members by taking the time to prepare for each session.

Accountability

The goal of the small-group experience is transformation. Each session helps learners identify aspects that need attention in their walk with Christ and their life as a believer, spouse, parent, and friend. Each week participants will be asked to consider courageous next steps. As a group, commit together to the accountability that is necessary to stay the course and live a courageous life.

SESSION 1
COURAGEOUS CALL

It takes COURAGE to fight for my FAMILY.

12

Do you know the name Rafael Peralta? Corporal Adam Morrison of the United States Marine Corps certainly does. On November 15, 2004, Rafael Peralta—a member of Morrison's unit—saved his life and "every Marine in that room."

Their unit had been cleansing Fallujah, Iraq, of terrorists "house by house" for seven days straight. That morning they entered a home and cleared the front rooms only to find a locked door on the left side. Sergeant Peralta opened the door to be met with gunfire from three terrorists with AK-47s. Peralta, alive but severely injured and lying on the floor in the doorway, noticed a grenade rolling into toward him. He grabbed the grenade and tucked it under his abdomen. When it exploded, he died, but the rest of his troop survived.

Peralta was a 25-year-old Mexican immigrant who enlisted in the Marines the day he received his green card. Leaving his parents for Iraq, he signed up to serve on the front lines. His bedroom at home contained three items on its walls: a copy of the Constitution, the Bill of Rights, and Peralta's certificate of graduation from boot camp.

SERGEANT PERALTA
April 7, 1979–November 15, 2004

His heroic act was foreshadowed by a note he wrote his younger brother, saying, "Be proud of me, bro. … and be proud of being an American." Those who know of Rafael Peralta can indeed be proud.[1]

It takes courage to enlist and sign up for frontline duty in an ongoing war. It takes courage to risk and voluntarily end your life for others and the perseverance of the mission. On the military battlefield, freedom is at stake. On the spiritual battlefield, our families are at stake and in danger. Our homes are under intense pressure and will become casualties unless we each answer the call to stand and fight for them.

Watch

MOVIE CLIP

View Clip 1, "Carjacking" (2:23), from the small-group DVD, and then use the discussion to start your study.

SUMMARY

In this scene, a man named Nathan Hayes pulls into a service station and begins pumping gas. Deciding to clean the dirt from his windshield, he steps away from the pump for a moment and a gang member steals his car. Much more concerned with the truck's contents than the truck itself, the action begins when Nathan risks everything to stop the thief. He is willing to lay down his life for what matters most to him, and the best thing he can do is keep his hands on the wheel.

OPEN DISCUSSION

As a group, do some basic introductions. Refresh everyone on the names and ages of your kids.

Danger and *fear* are words often associated with the word *courageous*. It takes courage to respond to a threatening situation. According to one popular description,

"COURAGE *is not the absence of fear, but rather the judgment that something else is more important than fear.*"[2]

1 Before you realized Nathan's objective, did you find yourself agreeing with his actions, or were you hoping he would give up? How did you feel once you realized what Nathan was fighting for?

Would you call his actions courageous and heroic? Why or why not?

2 Describe the most dangerous situation in which you ever found yourself. Would you react the same way now as you did then? Or, looking back, do you wish you had responded differently? Was your safety all that was at stake, or was someone else involved?

3 What scares you most about the life stages of your children? If you don't have kids, what concerns do you have about the possibility of one day being a parent?

4 What three things do you think most threaten families today? What sacrifices are you willing to make so these threats don't harm or destroy your family? How does courage help us make changes?

It's not unusual to be fearful about important people and important responsibilities. Yet Scripture teaches us that a better way is available on the path of life and parenting.

Study

The Book of Joshua begins with Moses' death and Joshua being named the newly appointed leader of God's people. Formerly, under Moses' leadership, Joshua led a victorious battle against the Amalekites (Ex. 17). Along with 11 others, Joshua spied the land of Canaan (Num. 13–14). Only he and Caleb came back with a favorable outlook toward the impending battle. Joshua's name means "The Lord is salvation" and corresponds with the New Testament name Jesus. Joshua was filled with the spirit, and now God was commissioning him for even greater service.

JOSHUA 1:1-9

1 After the death of Moses the LORD's servant, the LORD spoke to Joshua son of Nun, who had served Moses:

2 "Moses My servant is dead. Now you and all the people prepare to cross over the Jordan to the land I am giving the Israelites.

3 I have given you every place where the sole of your foot treads, just as I promised Moses.

4 Your territory will be from the wilderness and Lebanon to the great Euphrates River—all the land of the Hittites—and west to the Mediterranean Sea.

5 No one will be able to stand against you as long as you live. I will be with you, just as I was with Moses. I will not leave you or forsake you.

6 Be strong and courageous, for you will distribute the land I swore to their fathers to give them as an inheritance.

7 Above all, be strong and very courageous to carefully observe the whole instruction My servant Moses commanded you. Do not turn from it to the right or the left, so that you will have success wherever you go.

8 This book of instruction must not depart from your mouth; you are to recite it day and night so that you may carefully observe everything written in it. For then you will prosper and succeed in whatever you do.

9 Haven't I commanded you: be strong and courageous? Do not be afraid or discouraged, for the LORD your God is with you wherever you go."

Note the number of times God instructed Joshua to be "strong and courageous." Why might Joshua have been afraid? Why is courage a key to being a good leader?

What did God *promise* Joshua in this passage (vv. 3,7,9)?

God promises to bless us and give us true success. He is faithful to keep His promises. Most of all, He promises us His presence wherever we go.

What did God *require* of Joshua in this passage (vv. 6-9)?
What did God say is the key to success (v. 8)?

If you knew God was commanding you to do something, was going to bless you if you did it, and would always be with you helping you succeed, would you be more courageous?

Is there something God has already told you to do for which you need to take courage, trust Him, and obey?

Read Deuteronomy 31:23.

What was Moses telling Joshua before he (Moses) died?

Give examples of modern-day commissions. Do we have a parallel for Christian leadership today? for fathers or mothers?

Specifically, what have you as a man been commissioned by God to do?

Read Joshua 1:16-18.

How did the response of the people toward Joshua confirm God's call in his life?

What did the people promise to do? How did the requirements of God in Joshua's leadership translate to the lives of the people?

Compare Joshua 1:7-8 with Joshua 1:16-18. What connections do you see?

First, God commanded Joshua to be obedient to the book of the Law and to the Word of God. Then the people who were under Joshua's care committed to the same. Although Joshua made mistakes as a leader, he continued to seek the Lord and to get back on track as a strong example to those he led.

As men and women of faith, *the COMMITMENT of the people God entrusts to us will only be as strong as our own.* This is true of other believers we lead and disciple. It is also true for the children we are charged to raise.

Everyone

We are a people who value measurements in life. We get grades as children and seek merit raises as adults. Measurements are useful tools.

God's call to leadership for Joshua was also a call for him to commit to read and to dwell on God's Word (Josh. 1:8). In this study you will be considering your personal commitment to God's Word. Rate yourself on a scale of 1 to 10 with 10 being *completely committed* and 1 being *walking far from God*, and answer, "Why did I give myself that rating?" This is for your own understanding, not to share.

Courage to Follow God's Word

1   2   3   4   5   6   7   8   9   1 0

What factors influenced this rating?

Obedience to God's Word

1   2   3   4   5   6   7   8   9   1 0

What factors influenced this rating?

Meditation on Scripture

1   2   3   4   5   6   7   8   9   1 0

What factors influenced this rating?

Success as a Christ Follower

1   2   3   4   5   6   7   8   9   1 0

What factors influenced this rating?

What kind of commitment to Christ do your children see in you?
What kind of sacrifices are you making to help your family obey God?

Summary

We can all stand to improve in consistently reading God's Word and obeying His voice. Like Joshua, you may need reminders to be strong and courageous. You may need to recall that God will help you lead your family and will never leave you as you obey Him. You may need His reminder that He is calling you to spiritually lead, guide, and protect those under your care. Your success in spiritual leadership of your family is directly tied to your commitment to the Word of God.

Write three steps you will take this week to better read God's Word and obey His voice.

Dads and Moms

Consider how God wants you to sacrifice your life for the sake of your family.

Consider how He wants you to be a hero in your home. Consider the threats that war at the doors of your children's hearts and lives every day. Sometimes they can be physical threats (yellow grenades and carjacks), but often they are spiritual ones.

For example, boys often face bullying or peer pressure at school. Starting very young, girls may face issues of body image and a sexually pervasive culture. Even a toddler faces threats. Identify threats you think of in this space.

Other dangers to your family are not as easily spotted. What about attitudes of bitterness toward your spouse or children (Heb. 12:15)? How could unresolved marriage issues hurt your children? Do you allow harmful Internet, TV, or movie content into your home? What about friends who pull your children away from God? Do hobbies or other activities keep you or your kids away from church involvement?

Many godly parents have been where you have yet to go. You can benefit from their wisdom and friendship. They can encourage and support you.

Constantly pray for courage to address in a godly way the threats to your children. Pray for each child as he or she faces these challenges. Intentionally spend more time with your kids, learning their day-to-day routines. Like Nathan, hang on tightly to the wheel!

Pray for the wisdom and boldness to step up and be the dad you need to be—to serve, lead, and protect your family. God is calling men and women to courageously follow Christ and His Word. He is calling us to make the sacrifices needed to fight for our faith, for our families, and for future generations.

It is time to answer the call.

1. Oliver North, "Hero in Fallujah: Marine Laid Himself on Top of Grenade to Save Rest of Squad." [online] 16 December 2004 [cited 5 January 2011]. Available from the Internet: http://www.humanevents.com/article.php?id=6062
2. "Ambrose Redmoon Quotes" [online] 1999-2010 [cited 5 January 2011]. Available from the Internet: http://thinkexist.com/quotes/ambrose_redmoon

COURAGEOUS PRIORITIES

It takes COURAGE to value what matters most.

Living Large has a new meaning as of July 2010. While entering a lottery is not advised, Allen and Violet Large of Nova Scotia, Canada, won 11.3 million dollars in one and gave all their winnings away to local churches, charities, hospitals, and even the local fire station. After taking care of family and friends, the couple set out to give away the remainder of the money. They told the *Toronto Star*, "What you've never had, you never miss."

Violet, who was suffering from cancer at the time and undergoing chemotherapy, felt compelled to give generously to local hospitals and to cancer research. Allen told the *Star* that the money meant nothing and that it was much more important that the two had each other.

Truro Daily News

ALLEN AND VIOLET LARGE

The Larges spoke openly about how the winnings had complicated their lives and had been as much a burden as a blessing.[1] Their generosity easily begs the question, "What is really important in life?"

Keeping up with the Joneses is a challenge for anyone. Comparison can lead to one of two things: aggression or depression. It can either lead you to aggressively pursue what you don't have in order to achieve status that in the end won't satisfy or will cause overwhelming depression as you shift your focus from life's blessings to unmet wants and desires.

What makes the Larges' generosity so newsworthy is that it is so uncommon. When we find people who understand what matters most, they stand out. It takes courage to be that different and to have your life set apart according to a different (higher) standard.

Watch

MOVIE CLIP

View Clip 2, "Javier Suit Scene" (1:28), from the small-group DVD, and use the discussion to start your study.

SUMMARY

In this scene Javier is trying on a brand-new suit. His wife and children are excited about how nice he looks. Money is tight so the suit is an obvious stretch for the family budget; Javier expresses misgivings about the cost. Carmen insists it was the right thing to do for this special occasion—the time Javier will commit to spiritually lead his family. Javier tells her that he feels like a very rich man, and Carmen confirms that he should. When it comes to the things that matter, Javier is indeed wealthy.

Javier and Carmen are a couple who understand what matters in life. They are much richer than one might suppose.

OPEN DISCUSSION

Jesus reminds us, "For where your treasure is, there your heart will be also" (Matt. 6:21). If you consider what you talk about, think about, and spend your time and money on, you will discover where your heart is right now. You will also discover what you treasure most.

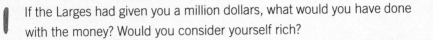

1   If the Larges had given you a million dollars, what would you have done with the money? Would you consider yourself rich?

2   How do our financial decisions reveal our values—what we think is most important?

3   What three things did Carmen identify in Javier's life that made him a true rich man?

4   In the space below, list five things in your life that matter most to you.

When we stop to consider what matters most in life, relationships usually make their way to the top of the list. Javier's relationships with God, his wife, and his children—those things that last—are what make him a rich man.

5   Why do you think we invest so much time and energy on things that do not last?

How would your life be different if you began prioritizing and living for the things that matter most to you?

Study

God's Word vividly illustrates the principle of wrong priorities. The city of Jericho had been burned (Josh. 6). God commanded that no one should take and keep the precious metals and ores of Jericho, but instead place them in the treasury of the Lord's house. If they obeyed, it would reveal that pleasing God was more important to them than possessing worldly treasures.

God was with Joshua and Israel just as He had promised. His specific instructions spread. Then it happened. Joshua 7:1 tells the story of Achan and the anger of the Lord imposed on the Israelites as the result of his sin.

JOSHUA 7:1

The Israelites, however, were unfaithful regarding the things set apart for destruction. Achan son of Carmi, son of Zabdi, son of Zerah, of the tribe of Judah, took some of what was set apart, and the Lord's anger burned against the Israelites.

What did Achan do that was so terrible?

What did God do in response to Achan's sin?

Read Joshua 7:2-12.

How did Joshua respond to God right after the battle of Ai (vv. 7-9)?

Read Joshua 7:19-21.

Why did Achan take from the articles consecrated to the Lord?

Why do you think Achan's sin stood out enough for God to teach the people such a strong lesson?

God judged the nation based on the sins of just one individual. He removed His hand of blessing because Achan, without the knowledge of all Israel or their senior leader, acted in disobedience to God. There was sin in the camp, and it had to be removed.

One failing grade is enough to bring down an entire GPA. One act of infidelity is enough to break apart a family. One single sin of omission or commission can have effects on your life and the life of your family for generations. In the case of Achan, it was a sin of value. He was tempted by the treasures of the world and chose them over obedience to the Lord.

JESUS SAID IT BEST:
"But collect for yourselves treasures in heaven, where neither moth nor rust destroys, and where thieves don't break in and steal. For where your treasure is, there your heart will be also."
Matthew 6:20-21

One misplaced value can be all the sin needed in the life of your family for Satan to grab a foothold. Achan coveted the things of the world more than the richness of God's promise. In reality, the things he coveted did not satisfy him. He couldn't even enjoy the spoils of the treasure; he had to hide them in order to have them. That certainly isn't satisfaction.

How does the world tempt you to place value on material wealth more than on Christ?

Share a time when something you thought was very satisfying turned out not to satisfy at all. What things other than God do you look to for satisfaction?

Does the philosophy of "keeping up with the Joneses" ever take hold of your family?

How does the current economic climate have you wanting more or fearfully holding on to what you have?

Read Joshua 7:24-26.

Achan's entire family suffered and died because of what he had done to Israel. This death sentence was legal under God's law and not only established justice but warned the entire nation to not make the same mistake and instead always to keep God first.

Are we allowing hidden sin in our lives? Do we really think it will *not* affect our families?

How can we literally stamp sin out of our lives today?

Achan confessed his sin, but Scripture does not state that he repented of it. Look at the actions of Joshua when he heard of the sin in Joshua 7:6 and contrast that with the attitude of Achan who merely stated the facts (7:20).

How is repentance from sin like putting it to death in our lives?

Anytime our selfish desires take priority over God's Word in our lives, we sin. That sin has powerful implications for our spiritual health as well as the condition of our family's spiritual health.

When we desire the things of this world more than the things of God, we open up our lives and our family to dissatisfaction and ultimately to the consequences of our actions. Misplaced values mean displaced lives.

"Do not love the world or the things that belong to the world.
If anyone loves the world, love for the Father is not in him.
For everything that belongs to the world—the lust of the flesh,
the lust of the eyes, and the pride in one's lifestyle—is not from
the Father, but is from the world. And the world with its lust is
passing away, but the one who does God's will remains forever."

1 John 2:15-17

Everyone

With the favor of God renewed among His people, the armies of Israel went on to defeat Ai in dramatic fashion. In response to their success, Joshua erected an altar and the people worshiped God through the reading and hearing of God's Word. Continue evaluating your commitment to God's Word as you read (or write out, if you prefer) the following verses of Scripture.

Joshua 1:7

Psalm 1:1-2

John 14:21

Summary

God commands us to keep His words. It is the key to success and the source of our happiness and delight. It is an indication of our love for Him and a direct link to further revelation from Him. It is the road of being blessed.

Write a sentence of renewed commitment to God. Remember, obedience to God is of the greatest value in life. What we value indicates our level of love and obedience to God.

Dads and Moms

Consider how God wants you to reprioritize your family's values. Discern how He wants you to lead and help script what matters to your sons and daughters.

1. Evaluate the world's attempts to entice your children with material things and Satan's ploys to create "sin in your camp" at home.

How has a misplaced focus on self kept you from freely giving from what God has given you? How have priorities regarding time kept you from serving?

How can you lead your family to desire the things of God?

Take a moment to identify misplaced values in your family. For example, how does the way you observe birthdays, Easter, and Christmas reinforce materialism rather than gratefulness to God for what He has done for you?

2. Remember what Carmen said to Javier. She spoke of three things that described great value and made Javier a very rich man.

How can you help reshape what your family views as true wealth?

On a separate piece of paper if needed, try to script three new values for yourself and your family. For example: "Turn off the TV and spend time as a family." "Get rid of things in our home that are weakening our spiritual lives." "Volunteer as a family to serve others."

Lastly, pray that God will give you the courage to value and prioritize what really matters.

1. "What you've never had, you never miss" [online] 5 November 2010 [cited 5 January 2011]. Available from the Internet: *http://www.dailymail.co.uk/news/article-1326473/Canadian-couple-Allen-Violet-Large-away-entire-11-2m-lottery-win.html*

COURAGEOUS
LEGACY

It takes
COURAGE
to impact future
generations.

President George H. W. Bush → President George W. Bush

Reverend Billy Graham → Reverend Franklin Graham

Archie Manning → Peyton, Eli Manning

The expression "Like father, like son" has many famous examples. The fathers mentioned have many reasons to be proud of their footstep-walking sons. While many children take roads completely different from their parents, we probably all know some who sadly have mirrored harmful ways and examples left by their parents as well.

Think for a moment about your own father and the patterns you hope to repeat—and those you hope to leave behind. Many of us, whether we like it or not, when it comes to raising kids of our own, we seem destined to repeat the same patterns of our own parents. In many cases, that's great. In other cases, it is not. As we parent children, a good question to ask is what personal characteristics we would be excited to see being instilled in our future grand-children. If there are things we think/believe/do that we would be alarmed by our kids' repeating, we would do well to reconsider our courses.

Perhaps the problems lie in waiting for those patterns to emerge naturally, as if fate has something to say rather than intentionally following Christ and modeling Him in our homes. Leaving a legacy starts with looking back and then setting a clear plan for going forward.

Billy Graham holding his young son, Franklin

What we learn very naturally growing up can easily translate to healthy or unhealthy patterns of behavior in our adult lives. It takes courage to walk a different path. It takes courage to break cycles. It takes courage to choose and to leave a legacy that will still matter for many generations to come.

Watch

MOVIE CLIP

View Clip 3, "Grill out/What was your dad like?" (2:40), from the small-group DVD, and use the discussion to start your study.

SUMMARY

In this scene, Adam and the guys are doing what guys do—grilling out! Adam is dealing with very specific challenges as a father and seeking wisdom about how to be a better dad. The lazy afternoon conversation takes a serious turn when the guys all share about the relationships they had with their own fathers.

OPEN DISCUSSION

Dad stories … we all have them, both good and bad. The men in the clip articulated theirs in just a few sentences. Take a few moments to express your own dad story.

1 What impact has your father's presence or absence had on you? How has he influenced your faith, your family, and your choices in life?

(Nathan mentions the profound effect his father's absence had in his life and also the positive influence of another man who stepped into the gap for him. If you lost your dad at a young age, describe the effects of the loss but also feel free to talk/write about the stepdad or father figure in your life.)

2 As part of your dad-story exercise, identify which of the four men in the clip you relate to most (circle or check). Was it—

Nathan, with the absentee father but positive mentor?
Shane, with the dad who didn't practice what he preached?
David, whose dad left after infidelity and the home was never the same?
Adam, who had a good dad, leaving no failures worth mentioning?

3 As a group, take time to share your dad stories with each other. How have your father's decisions impacted your life? Try to be as open and transparent as possible.

4 What are the positive elements of your family of origin that you are trying to keep strong in your own family?

5 With what negative elements from your family of origin do you struggle to break the chains?

Study

Much of the Book of Joshua is about tribal territories. Each of the clans, named for the sons of Jacob, was given portions of the promised land as an inheritance. Violent nations filled with pagan idolatry, child sacrifice, and endless immorality had been driven out and replaced by God's people. The promises God made as far back as Genesis 12 were being fulfilled in the life of Joshua's Israel. For Old Testament Israel, the legacy of their forefathers came packaged in the promise of land.

In Joshua 23, an aging Joshua gives a final address to the people of God. His life and leadership left a powerful legacy, and the words in his final farewell add intentionality to the mark he made. Carefully read this account.

JOSHUA 23:1-10

1 A long time after the Lord had given Israel rest from all the enemies around them, Joshua was old, getting on in years.

2 So Joshua summoned all Israel, including its elders, leaders, judges, and officers, and said to them, "I am old, getting on in years,

3 and you have seen for yourselves everything the Lord your God did to all these nations on your account, because it was the Lord your God who was fighting for you.

4 See, I have allotted these remaining nations to you as an inheritance for your tribes, including all the nations I have destroyed, from the Jordan westward to the Mediterranean Sea.

5 The Lord your God will force them back on your account and drive them out before you so that you can take possession of their land, as the Lord your God promised you.

6 Be very strong and continue obeying all that is written in the book of the law of Moses, so that you do not turn from it to the right or left

7 and so that you do not associate with these nations remaining among you. Do not call on the names of their gods or make an oath to them; do not worship them or bow down to them.

8   Instead, remain faithful to the LORD your God, as you have done
    to this day.

9   The LORD has driven out great and powerful nations before you,
    and no one is able to stand against you to this day.

10 One of you routed a thousand because the LORD your God was
    fighting for you, as He promised."

What words in this passage seem familiar to you? (Reference Josh. 1.)

How had God accomplished for Israel what He promised (v. 10)?

Read Joshua 23:11-13.

How had this warning already been reality for the people of God? (Reference
Josh. 7.) Continue with Joshua's farewell speech.

JOSHUA 23:14-16

14 "I am now going the way of all the earth, and you know with all
    your heart and all your soul that none of the good promises the
    LORD your God made to you has failed. Everything was fulfilled for
    you; not one promise has failed.

15 Since every good thing the LORD your God promised you has come
    about, so He will bring on you every bad thing until He has annihi-
    lated you from this good land the LORD your God has given you.

16 If you break the covenant of the LORD your God, which He
    commanded you, and go and worship other gods, and bow down
    to them, the LORD's anger will burn against you, and you will
    quickly disappear from this good land He has given you."

What did Joshua *remind* the people of in verse 14?

What did Joshua *warn* the people about in verses 15-16?

Everyone

Joshua used his legacy speech to remind the people of God's faithfulness and to warn the people of God's response to their unfaithfulness. A good legacy of faith both reminds and warns future generations. Whether it is a good example with rewards or a bad example with consequences, we can learn a lot from those who have gone before us.

Based on these terms, who has left the best legacy of faith in your life?

How did this person's life and words include both a *reminder* and a *warning* for you and your faith?

Consider the impact your biological dad has had on your life. Whether by his absence or his presence, he has left a considerable mark.

Before you can actively take part in leaving a positive legacy for the next generation of your family, you have to unpack and deal with the legacy left in your life.

While none of our earthly fathers are perfect, many of them have made much of Christ with their words and actions and made incredible spiritual invest-ments in our lives. However, many suffer significant scars from a father who left or a dad who was around but whose actions brought hurt and unrest.

If your father's legacy was largely positive, continue with Part A before going to the Summary section. If your father's legacy was largely negative, skip to Part B and then conclude with the Summary section. First, watch a clip highlighting some contemporary experiences related to legacy building.

Watch

View Clip 4, "Sherwood Dads Share Parenting Experiences" (6:15), before moving into your time of application.

THE SHERWOOD DADS
Jim McBride, Stephen Kendrick, Michael Catt, Alex Kendrick

PART A: If your father left a worthwhile spiritual legacy in your life, write down the most important lessons and warnings he spoke into your life. These are offerings you will strive for in your own legacy.

Commit this week to contacting your dad and expressing your gratitude for his faithful legacy. Offer to him the specifics of his investments in your life, and tell how each one continues to impact your walk with Christ and leadership in your family.

If your dad is no longer with you, consider writing a prayer of thanks to God for your dad. Keep it in your Bible as a reminder of God's favor in your life and to invest the same in the lives of others.

PART B: If your father left a wealth of pain in his wake, moving forward will require healing and health. Both require forgiveness.

In *COURAGEOUS*, Nathan learns to work through the hurts from his father and forgive him. This is a vital step in breaking past chains and moving forward. Healing does not begin until forgiveness takes place (Mark 11:25). Forgiveness allows us to turn all the anger and hurt over to God so He can be the Judge and deal with those who have wounded us (Rom. 12:17-19).

If you are ready to be free from any bitterness with your father, write down a statement of pain caused by his past actions. Then follow it with a declaration of your choice to be like Jesus and grant your dad complete forgiveness. Pray and tell God of your choice to forgive your father. Ask Him to break the chains in your heart. Write FORGIVEN across this page.

Finally, if you feel ready to do so, consider contacting your dad and expressing your desire to begin rebuilding your relationship. Apologize if you have also hurt him in the past. If your dad is no longer with you, consider writing a letter of forgiveness to him. Keep it with you as a reminder of God's healing power in your life and to break the cycles of sin in your future family.

Summary

Before we can choose the legacy we leave to others, we have to fully consider the ones left in us. By forgiving and learning from their lives, we can move forward with strength. Perhaps you have started out on shaky ground with your spiritual investment. As long as you have life and breath, you can change the impact you make. Even if you had a lousy legacy from your earthly father, you can cling to a perfect legacy of faith from your Heavenly Father who has, according to Joshua 23:14, fulfilled every promise He has ever made.

Dads and Moms

Consider the legacy you want to leave for your kids. Consider the legacy your life is already leaving by the things you say and do and the way you represent God in word and deed. Ask God to help you identify those things you are doing well and those areas in which you need to improve—for your sake and for the sake of future generations.

My positive legacy:

1.

2.

3.

My commitment to change:

1.

2.

3.

Pray now for courage to boldly leave a legacy of faith in your family. The greatest impact you have on your children will be how you love God and love your spouse.

The direction of your kids' *dating, marriage, career, service, leadership, faithfulness* to God and His church, and ultimately their *parenting* will be a direct reflection of you and the marks you leave in their lives.

If that sounds frightening, that's because it is. It is an incredible responsibility, and doing it with success will take courage! Be strong and courageous!

COURAGEOUS FAITH

It takes COURAGE to stand WITH CHRIST.

Only in recent years has the name Steve Saint rung any bells. Steve was the five-year-old son of Nate Saint, the missionary pilot who died alongside Jim Elliot and three other missionaries in 1956 at the hands of the Waodani (whoa-DONNY) tribe in Ecuador. At age nine, Steve returned to the Waodani

territory for the first time. As a young man, Saint began a long-lasting friendship with Mincaye (min-KY-yee), one of the men who killed his father. "What the Waodani meant for evil, God used for good," says Steve.[1]

The stories of Elisabeth Elliot and Rachel Saint have long been associated with forgiveness. What better picture of grace and mercy than that of a missionary widow and sister to return and share good news with the very people who murdered their family members?

Steve Saint with Mincaye

Perhaps there is no greater illustration of forgiveness than the forged relationship between a son and the tribal murderer who took his dad. Here we see vividly illustrated the life-changing gospel of Jesus that Jim, Nate, and the other missionaries set out to share in the first place.

Jim Elliot wrote in his journal, "He is no fool who gives what he cannot keep to gain that which he cannot lose."[2]

The apostle Paul wrote in his Letter to the Philippians, "My eager expectation and hope is that I will not be ashamed about anything, but that now as always, with all boldness, Christ will be highly honored in my body, whether by life or by death. For me, living is Christ and dying is gain" (Phil. 1:20-21).

When choosing to stand with Jesus, the stakes are always high. The question is not what you lose by standing with Him but what you will lose if you do not.

Watch

MOVIE CLIP

View Clip 5, "Gospel Presentation at Gun Range" (3:40), from the small-group DVD, and use the discussion to start your study.

SUMMARY

In this scene Nathan seizes an opportunity to share his faith with his rookie partner, David. When David asks Nathan about the importance of fathers, Nathan realizes that David's concerns go much deeper than the question indicates. Nathan shares an allegory that helps the young officer understand Christ's saving grace. Recognizing his own sin and guilt, David admits that he is tired of feeling guilty.

Nathan speaks the gospel, and David responds. What will David do with his new understanding?

OPEN DISCUSSION

Whether related to fear of death, fear of controversy, fear of failing, or some other fear, we consider courage a prerequisite when it comes to actively sharing the gospel.

 As a group, take time to briefly share your own faith story. Who introduced you to Jesus?

 Now consider those with whom you have never shared how to have a relationship with Christ. What is at stake if they never hear the gospel?

3 What was your first reaction to hearing how Nathan opened the door and shared Christ with David? What seemed natural to you? What seemed difficult?

4 Nathan didn't create an opportunity to share Christ as much as he seized one. How did Nathan balance truth with kindness in how he shared with David?

What day-to-day opportunities do you have to begin sharing Christ?

5 How actively are you seeking to share Christ with your children (age appropriately)? Or are you trusting the church to do it for you?

6 God's Word commands parents to lead and teach their children spiritually (Deut. 6:1-7). How openly do you discuss spiritual matters in your own home?

"Honor the Messiah as Lord in your hearts. Always be ready to give a defense to anyone who asks you for a reason for the hope that is in you."
1 Peter 3:15

The final chapter of Joshua is a continuation of the leader's address that began in chapter 23. It contains one of the most frequently referenced verses about the family (Josh. 24:15) and sets up Israel's continued story as told in the Book of Judges.

Whereas Moses, by God's power, led the people out of Egypt, Joshua led them into Canaan. Both leaders endured hard seasons of wilderness wanderings, and in the end Joshua courageously claimed the prize that was promised to Abraham, Isaac, and Jacob.

JOSHUA 24:1-13

1 Joshua assembled all the tribes of Israel at Shechem and summoned Israel's elders, leaders, judges, and officers, and they presented themselves before God.

2 Joshua said to all the people, "This is what the LORD, the God of Israel, says: 'Long ago your ancestors, including Terah, the father of Abraham and Nahor, lived beyond the Euphrates River and worshiped other gods.

3 But I took your father Abraham from the region beyond the Euphrates River, led him throughout the land of Canaan, and multiplied his descendants. I gave him Isaac,

4 and to Isaac I gave Jacob and Esau. I gave the hill country of Seir to Esau as a possession, but Jacob and his sons went down to Egypt.

5 'Then I sent Moses and Aaron; I plagued Egypt by what I did there and afterward I brought you out.

6 When I brought your fathers out of Egypt and you reached the Red Sea, the Egyptians pursued your fathers with chariots and horsemen as far as the sea.

7 Your fathers cried out to the LORD, so He put darkness between you and the Egyptians, and brought the sea over them, engulfing them. Your own eyes saw what I did to Egypt. After that, you lived in the wilderness a long time.

8 'Later, I brought you to the land of the Amorites who lived beyond the Jordan. They fought against you, but I handed them over to you. You possessed their land, and I annihilated them before you.

9 Balak son of Zippor, king of Moab, set out to fight against Israel. He sent for Balaam son of Beor to curse you,

10 but I would not listen to Balaam. Instead, he repeatedly blessed you, and I delivered you from his hand.

11 'You then crossed the Jordan and came to Jericho. The people of Jericho—as well as the Amorites, Perizzites, Canaanites, Hittites, Girgashites, Hivites, and Jebusites—fought against you, but I handed them over to you.

12 I sent the hornet ahead of you, and it drove out the two Amorite kings before you. It was not by your sword or bow.

13 I gave you a land you did not labor for, and cities you did not build, though you live in them; you are eating from vineyards and olive groves you did not plant.'"

What did God say about Himself to His people in this passage?

Why is it important to periodically be reminded of an historical account of God's work in our lives?

What specific activity of God in the life of His people from Abraham to Joshua do you find particularly exciting? What part of the Israelite story speaks most to you and why?

JOSHUA 24:14-15, NIV

14 "Now fear the Lord and serve him with all faithfulness. Throw away the gods your forefathers worshiped beyond the River and in Egypt, and serve the Lord.

15 But if serving the Lord seems undesirable to you, then choose for yourselves this day whom you will serve, whether the gods your forefathers served beyond the River, or the gods of the Amorites, in whose land you are living. But as for me and my household, we will serve the Lord."

What do Joshua's final words say about his own leadership of his home?

Why was it important that Joshua speak for his entire house?

Knowing what you know about Joshua, do you think he would have carried out his commitment even if he were the only one? What about you?

JOSHUA 24:16-18

16 The people replied, "We will certainly not abandon the Lord to worship other gods!

17 For the Lord our God brought us and our fathers out of the land of Egypt, out of the place of slavery, and performed these great signs before our eyes. He also protected us all along the way we went and among all the peoples whose lands we traveled through.

18 The Lord drove out before us all the peoples, including the Amorites who lived in the land. We too will worship the Lord, because He is our God."

How did the people respond to Joshua's call?

How did Joshua's narrative retelling of God's faithfulness affect how the people thought and responded?

Hundreds of years later, in his address to the Hellenistic Jews in Acts 7, Stephen used the same method to share his faith by recounting the history of Israel from Abraham to Solomon. He challenged their belief in the earthly temple for the sake of Christ's temple and proclaimed Jesus as the fulfillment of God's promise. Stephen laid down his life for Christ and was stoned for his courageous faith, becoming the first Christian martyr. The gospel he shared not only impacted those in his day but also spread around the world.

By recounting God's faithfulness throughout history and our own lives, we can create a strong "apologetic" argument of the gospel for the lost to hear. *Apologetics* refers to a branch of theological study aimed at providing a defense for God and for one's faith in Christ. It comes from the Greek word a*pologia,* which means to give a verbal defense for one's opinion against an attack. It is the word translated "defense" in 1 Peter 3:15 (p. 45).

Our response to Jesus Christ being Lord of our lives is to share who He is and what He has done. The apologetic argument often involves a narrative approach to faith sharing. The apostle Paul used this approach by recounting the complete story of how Christ changed his life and called him to salvation.

What was the significance of Joshua's or Stephen's historical recounting of God's faithfulness dating back to Abraham?

How is the entire faith story important when it comes to boldly sharing one's faith?

What advantages do you see in using a narrative approach in sharing Christ?

Look back at the first part of 1 Peter 3:15. How is honoring Christ as Lord in your heart good preparation for God to make you a witness for His name?

Everyone

Consider the God of the universe and His pronounced judgment on sin. Consider His love, that He would create an alternative to such punishment by the death of His own Son, Jesus.

Joshua contended the same. The people were slaves in Egypt, and God sent a savior. God blessed the Old Testament Israelites by giving them the land He promised. And He blesses us by offering us the promise of eternal life if we will repent of our sins and place our total faith in His Son, Jesus.

If you have not settled this today, in the words of Nathan, "What is holding you back?" Make the choice to trust Christ today. Page 53 walks you through simple steps to trusting Christ. Turn there now.

If you have trusted Christ for eternity, what is holding you back from boldly seizing opportunities to share the hope you have with others?

Summary

It takes the fullness of the Holy Spirit working in our lives for us to see the opportunities to share Christ that present themselves every day. It also takes courage to act and seize those opportunities as they come.

Christ is best shared in the context of relationship. Nathan and David were already friends. They were partners at work. After David's decision, they would be brothers in Christ for life.

Write the names of three people with whom you already have a relationship and can share your hope in Christ this week.

1.

2.

3.

As you await the right moment, pray: "Heavenly Father, I thank You for those You sent into my life to share how I could have a relationship with You through Christ. Please make me an effective soul winner and equip me with the gospel of peace so I can boldly share the good news as well. In Jesus' name, amen."

Be prepared, in season and out, to share Christ. Confidently pray, asking God to open doors; conduct yourself with wisdom when you are with nonbelievers; and tailor your speech to the situation (Col. 4:2-3).

Dads and Moms

It took courage for Joshua to stand with God despite the wickedness of the people, and it takes courage to stand with Christ today. There are many faiths and religions out there, and Jesus said that if we stand for Him we will be rejected by the world. But our strong witness for Christ will not only honor God but also draw the lost to salvation.

In what ways does your family need to unapologetically take a stand for Christ? It may be as simple as making church participation a priority over sports. It may be as deep and difficult as openly sharing Christ with a neighborhood family who is antagonistic to faith.

If you are a mom or dad of older children, ask yourself if you have been a strong example of keeping Christ first before your children. If not, isn't it time to step up and stand firm with Christ in your conversations? This may mean owning up to your part in allowing other things to prevent Christ from being first place in your home. Pray for courage as you boldly share with your children the hope you have found in Jesus.

Perhaps as a mom or dad of young children you are working to lay a foundation for faith so that one day your kids will choose Christ. Satan does not want you to be successful. You likely are already experiencing the attacks of a world that would deter your resolve. Courageously renew your commitment today. As for you and your house, determine to worship and serve the Lord.

Perhaps your family needs to actively share Christ with other family members and close friends. Identify those today who need to see and hear the gospel narrative from you and your family. Specify those individuals you will invite to church with you this week. Be willing to help your children do the same, even if it means driving out of your way to pick up their friends.

Take time this week to lead your family in a discussion about faith sharing. Talk about it daily. Decide as a family the people you would like to share with, and pray as a family for each person. Write down names and pray for opportunities for each member of your family to courageously stand with and share Jesus.

In the COURAGEOUS clip we viewed, Nathan made his case and asked David, "What's holding you back from settling this today?" Scripture tells us how Joshua made his case for God and called the people to choose, based on the reputation of God, whom they would worship. Then Joshua pronounced that he and his house would worship the Lord.

After all that Christ did for us, who would choose otherwise?

1. "Steve Saint: The Legacy of the Martyrs" [online] n.d. [cited 5 January 2011]. Available from the Internet: http://www.cbn.com/700club/Guests/Bios/steve_saint010305.aspx
2. "Jim Elliot Quote" [online] 2008 [cited 5 January 2011]. Available from the Internet: http://www.wheaton.edu/bgc/archives/faq/20.htm

A New Life

The Bible tells us that our hearts tend to run from God and rebel against Him. The Bible calls this "sin." *Romans 3:23 says, "For all have sinned and fall short of the glory of God."* Every lie, bitter response, selfish attitude, and lustful thought separates us from God. We all deserve His judgment.

Even though you deserve judgment, God loves you and wants to save you from sin and offer you a new life of hope. *John 10:10 says, "I [Jesus] have come that they may have life and have it in abundance."*

To give you this gift of salvation, God made a way by sending His Son, Jesus Christ. *Romans 5:8 tells us, "But God proves His own love for us in that while we were still sinners, Christ died for us!"*

You receive this gift by faith alone. *Ephesians 2:8 says, "For you are saved by grace through faith, and this is not from yourselves; it is God's gift."*

Faith is a decision of your heart demonstrated by the actions of your life. *Romans 10:9 says, "If you confess with your mouth, 'Jesus is Lord,' and believe in your heart that God raised Him from the dead, you will be saved."* The Bible commands everyone to repent and to believe on the Lord Jesus Christ to be saved. If you choose right now to believe Jesus died for your sins and to receive new life through Him, consider praying a prayer like this:

> "Dear God, I confess that I am a sinner and that my sin separates me from You. I believe Jesus died to forgive me of my sins. I accept Your offer of eternal life. Thank You for forgiving me of all my sin and giving me my new life. From this day forward, I will choose to follow You."

If you prayed such a prayer, share your decision with a Christian friend or pastor. If you are not already attending church, find one that preaches the Bible and will help you worship and grow in your faith. Following Christ's example, ask to be baptized by immersion as a public expression of your faith.

The What, Who, How, and Why of Accountability
Nic Allen

Google™ the word *accountability*. The top 10 hits (after Wikipedia® and Merriam-Webster®) will likely include articles or sites dealing with fiscal responsibility, corporate integrity, and product reliability. The personal account-ability of the Christ follower is something similar yet different altogether.

While Scripture doesn't explicitly mention accountability, its urgency is implicit particularly in passages describing successful Christian community. So what exactly is accountability? How do we do it? To whom should we be accountable and why?

The What

One day we all will stand before God to give an account for who we are and how we have lived. Scripture references the judgment seat of God in numerous passages. Trusting Christ for salvation will be all that matters when we meet our Maker.

Becoming a Christian by believing in Christ is very easy. But when it comes to following Him, we often flounder. Accountability is a discipleship tool that operates in the context of relationships. It is one friend helping another to live for Christ and holding another to a standard of faith and vice versa.

The Who

Several essentials can be identified for successful accountability relationships.

1. Faith. Both parties must be people of expressed faith in Christ. While it is important to develop influential relationships with nonbelievers, accountability is best in a relationship yoked by Jesus.

2. Homogeny. Both parties must be of the same gender. There is a world of difference between how men and women communicate and relate to the world. Men and women deal with different temptations and pressures.

Entering into an accountability relationship with a member of the opposite sex (other than the one to whom you are married) could lead to a level of intimacy that births physical attraction. That is an unhealthy temptation. While there is certainly a call for accountability in a marriage relationship, each spouse should also seek the accountability of a friend of the same sex to walk with them through life's challenges and maintain fidelity in their marriage.

3. Shared struggle. Perhaps it makes sense to find someone to hold you accountable in areas in which you struggle but they do not. But who better to help you toe the line than someone who needs the same encouragement? When your accountability partner struggles in the same area you do, he likely understands the temptation and knows intimately the signs of weakness and the weight of consequences. The shared struggle can be a shared incentive.

The success of 12-step programs is due in part to sponsorship relationships. Sponsors may be people further down the road of recovery, but they always understand the struggle firsthand. Who better to hold you accountable in daily Bible reading than someone who also needs to be asked about his personal time with God? Who better to hold someone accountable in struggles with morality than someone else who knows firsthand the dangers of the sin?

The Why

Dozens of biblical mandates and illustrations come to mind when considering our need for accountable relationships. None are quite as obvious as the wisdom of Solomon in Ecclesiastes and of James in the New Testament.

> "Two are better than one because they have a good reward for their efforts. For if either falls, his companion can lift him up; but pity the one who falls without another to lift him up. Also, if two lie down together, they can keep warm; but how can one person alone keep warm? And if somebody overpowers one person, two can resist him. A cord of three strands is not easily broken."—**Ecclesiastes 4:9-12**

> "Therefore, confess your sins to one another and pray for one another, so that you may be healed. The urgent request of a righteous person is very powerful in its effect."—**James 5:16**

The How

So how do you do accountability? Here are some steps to get you started on a successful road to healthy accountability.

1. **Identify an accountability partner.** Both parties must agree to be honest about struggles and to sharing the load of carrying another brother.

2. **Select the frequency and methodology of your accountability relationship.** Decide whether to meet weekly face to face or have several phone check-in times. Determine a method for outside communication.

3. **Agree on honesty and confidentiality.** Both parties must agree to be honest and to keep what is shared completely confidential in order to build and maintain trust.

4. **Pray for one another.** James said that confession is only part of the process. The other half is prayer, the most powerful medium for the faithful Christian.

5. **Spur one another on toward Christ.** The writer of Hebrews discouraged us from abandoning our gatherings with other believers (Heb. 10:25) but to instead encourage one another toward love and good deeds. Accountability shouldn't ever be just about that from which we abstain. It should also be about the values we work to incorporate into daily Christlike living.

Done right and given the proper place in our lives, accountability can prove to be the most mutually beneficial relationship in our lives. Any covenant relationship where people are honest about sin and committed to prayer is bound to enjoy the favor of God and the success of following Christ better every day.

Courage to Keep Commitments

A movie-release curriculum *Honor Begins at Home: The COURAGEOUS Bible Study* (item 005371686, fall 2011) can take men or couples deeper into concepts of this Bible study. Through this follow-up, men can grow in courage to keep commitments to God, their spouses, and their children as they walk "doubly accountable" to God and other believers. *The Resolution for Men* and *The Resolution for Women* are accompanying resources.

Leader Notes
Small-Group Quick Tips

1. Distribute the responsibility.
As a leader, the temptation is always to do everything personally; that quickly leads to frustration. Your main focus is to prepare the lesson in advance and prioritize the most important aspects during class discussion. Divvy maintenance tasks such as keeping track of attendance, prayer request follow-up, and refreshment sign-ups. In group meetings, ask different learners to read Scripture and sections of content and to lead out in group discussion.

2. Make the group a safe place.
Remind your group weekly as you engage in open discussion about the sensitivity of things people may share. Keep confidentiality and respect in focus.

3. Set the pace.
As a leader, you set the pace for your group. Your willingness to share and be transparent will have a direct impact on others' willingness to do the same. Your advance preparation and commitment to start and end on time will influence the group's direction. Your desire to stay on task and not chase rabbits will indicate what is appropriate and inappropriate in terms of group dynamics.

4. Be comfortable with silent moments and unanswered questions.
Often silence creates discomfort for a leader who may feel pressure to fill the awkwardness by talking more. As a leader, be OK with long pauses. Sometimes this is just an indication that the question has warranted more thought.

Some people may present difficult life challenges. Often they aren't looking for answers as much as a listening ear. Be sensitive but guide conversations to stay focused. Sometimes you may only recognize the difficulty of the situation and acknowledge the need to seek the Lord when answers are not clear.

5. Pray for your group members.
Oswald Chambers has said, "Prayer does not fit us for the greater work; prayer is the greater work."[1] How you commit to praying for your group is much more

valuable than how well you lead your group. In fact, how well you lead will be a direct reflection of how well you pray for the people in your group.

Commit to pray for the people God has entrusted to you, that they will:
- have eyes that are open to see God move
- have ears that hear the Word and commit to doing what it says
- genuinely repent of sin as the Holy Spirit convicts them through God's Word
- grow spiritually and begin to develop a daily intimate walk with the Lord
- make wise choices
- be committed to the group study
- live lives of integrity in their homes, communities, and places of work
- lead their children well
- be committed to their spouses
- trust Christ in any and all circumstances of life
- be free from temptation and the attacks of the enemy
- take on the full armor of God as both their defense and offense in the spiritual battles they face
- love God supremely and love others well

Optional Group Icebreakers

My Story

Ask learners to recount a significant moment in their lives using ideas from the following list. If you have couples in your group, you may want to ask them to share together the story of how they met and married.

To whom are you married? How did you meet?

What do you do? How did you choose that career?

What are your kids' names? How and why did you choose those names?

Where are you from? How and why did you or your family move here?

Who are your parents? What do or did they do in life?

Who are your siblings? Where do you fall in birth order? Who were you closest to growing up? Who are you closest to now?[2]

Snapshots

Help people get a glimpse of who you really are by writing or drawing snap-shots of yourself and telling your group the most interesting one(s). Depending on time and the number of people, complete one or more statements.

A time:
I was really happy …
I took a big chance and it paid off …
I toughed it out and accomplished a big goal …
I was really embarrassed …
I really chickened out …
I was in a rut …

My Stock Market

How many people hold stock in your life? How many invest in you? Who would suffer most if the "company of your life" filed for bankruptcy? Who would benefit most if your stock soared?

You have been given 1,000 shares. Indicate how this stock is currently distrib-uted and who owns how many shares of you:[3]

Spouse	_____	Shares
Children	_____	Shares
Parents	_____	Shares
Friends	_____	Shares
Workplace	_____	Shares
Other	_____	Shares

1. Taken from *My Utmost for His Highest* by Oswald Chambers. © l935 by Dodd Mead & Co., renewed © 1963 by the Oswald Chambers Publications Assn., Ltd., and is used by permis-sion of Discovery House Publishers, Box 3566, Grand Rapids MI 4950l. All rights reserved. Available from the Internet: *http://www.myutmost.org/10/1017.html*
2. Adapted from *Icebreakers and Heartwarmers: 101 Ways to Kick Off and End Meetings* by Steve Sheely (Nashville, TN: Serenity House Publishers, 1998), 67.
3. Ibid., 77.

Follow-Up Resources

COURAGEOUS

- *Honor Begins at Home: The COURAGEOUS Bible Study* (fall 2011 release, member, item 005371686; DVD leader kit, item 005325609) Eight-week study can serve as impetus for starting men's accountability groups and be used with movie
- *Courageous Living; The Resolution for Men/The Resolution for Women* (pp. 61,64)
- *http://www.LifeWay.com/Courageous, http://www.courageousthemovie.com*
- Also visit *www.dayspring.com/courageous* for additional resources.

PARENTING

- Life Truths Small Group Curriculum
  www.lifeway.com/lifetruths
- All Pro Dad: *www.allprodad.com*
- *The Parent Adventure: Preparing Your Children for a Lifetime with God* (7 sessions: member: item 005181385; DVD leader kit, item 005126524)
- *Raising Girls and Boys: The Art of Understanding Their Differences* (October 2011 release; 6 sessions: member, item 005260397; DVD leader kit, item 005324579)
- *HomeLife* magazine See monthly "Wise Guys" section just for men. To interact with other parents, visit *www.lifeway.com/homelifeonline*
- *ParentLife* magazine (available monthly; also quarterly bundles and subscriptions) To interact with other parents, visit *www.lifeway.com/parentlifeblog*

MEN'S MINISTRY

- *Game Plan for Life* (Vols. 1 and 2)
  www.lifeway.com/gameplan and *www.gameplanforlife.com*
  (Vol. 1: 6 sessions; member, item 005259409; DVD leader kit, item 005269065;
  Vol. 2: 6 sessions; member, item 005371575; DVD leader kit, item 005371574)
- Every Man Ministries: *www.everymanministries.com*
- Iron Sharpens Iron: *www.ironsharpensiron.net*
- *Stand Firm* magazine, a Christian devotional magazine for men

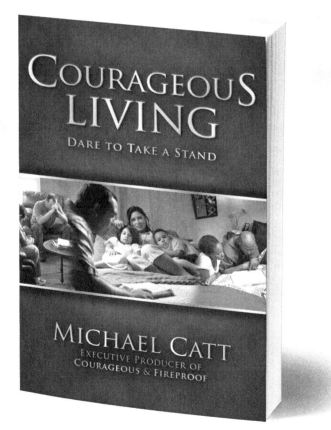

If you like the changes in your home now,

imagine what could happen if you go even deeper.

The 8-week *Honor Begins at Home: The COURAGEOUS Bible Study* will take individuals and small groups deeper into biblical truths for a godly family, exploring topics such as redeeming your history, walking with integrity, winning and blessing the hearts of your children, and more.

Each session uses movie clips to engage people in discussion. And daily readings from *The Resolution for Men* and *The Resolution for Women* will help you connect with God and His best plan for your family.

This study will be available in fall 2011. To order, call 800.458.2772 or visit www.lifeway.com/courageous

BRING THE POWER OF
COURAGEOUS
HOME TO YOUR FAMILY....
WITH "THE RESOLUTION"™ PRINT!

The first step men take is to be accountable to God and one another.

When a man signs his Resolution, he makes promises that will impact his life and his family for good for generations.

Visibly displaying the Resolution affirms a family's commitment to each other and the Lord.

Find "The Resolution"™ as seen in the movie in framed and unframed versions at your favorite Christian retail stores this September. Also available unframed in bulk quantities for your church and curriculum groups.

FOR MORE INFORMATION, GO TO
WWW.DAYSPRING.COM/COURAGEOUS

design may vary

DaySpring®
Your heart. God's love.

FROM THE CREATORS OF FIREPROOF
COURAGEOUS
HONOR BEGINS AT HOME
IN THEATERS SEPTEMBER 30

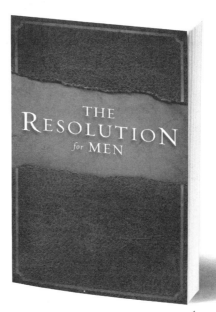

by Stephen & Alex
Kendrick
with Randy Alcorn

Inspiring a Revolution

by Priscilla Shirer
Foreword by Stephen
& Alex Kendrick

Available September 2011
IAmCourageous.com

BOOKS